HERB JACKSON
CORT SAVAGE
RUSS WARREN

An exhibition of recent work by the
studio art faculty of Davidson College

Essay by Richard Shiff

William H. Van Every, Jr. Gallery
Visual Arts Center
Davidson College, Davidson, North Carolina

CONTENTS

CRAFTING CONCENTRATION: Three Artists At Davidson   5

Herb Jackson   18

Cort Savage   32

Russ Warren   46

CRAFTING CONCENTRATION: Three Artists At Davidson

An exhibition should offer more than a group of individual objects, each competing for the viewer's attention. It can arrange its objects as complements to one another, intensifying and concentrating their effect. The structure of a college art department, with its curriculum, can do the same for the artists themselves. It concentrates their activity within a studio building housing them in their role as teachers, and also within a pedagogical program which guides their collective effort. When successful, colleges and exhibitions thus operate by the same principle: no matter how excellent the components may be as individuals, the whole creates situations and moments of reciprocal enhancement, so as to exceed the sum of its parts.

To speak of a concentration in this way is not to imply a uniformity of effect. The talents and expertise of a group of independent and engagingly idiosyncratic artists — brought together as a department, teaching together and exhibiting together — cannot create a collective style or "school" of art where none was intended. Herb Jackson, Cort Savage, and Russ Warren remain very different people with different artistic agenda. Their independently conceived forms nevertheless play off one another, generating cumulative force. This is so because these three artists at Davidson share something of an ethic — not a style or a technique, but rather a particular way of being creative, a way of acting out the role of the artist.

Given their differences, what, more particularly, could Jackson, Savage, and Warren possibly hold in common? At what point do their independent perspectives converge upon a shared course of action? The common element is a certain intensification and density, a concentration already present in their work, which becomes all the more obvious as one perceives this quality threefold. "Concentration" seems the right word to me; it comes to mind when I view the works, perhaps in part because I sense that the works are causing me to concentrate my own energies. But what does "concentration" mean? When is something concentrated?

To concentrate is to bring materials or forces — whether physical, intellectual, or psychological — to a center ("concentrate" and "concentric" share an etymology). Viewing the exhibited works of the Davidson faculty, and noting the artists' thoughts and observing their actions, I find a remarkable concentration of *craft*. This is not the kind of craft for which illustrators get contracted by the piece or the hour, or for which a jeweler gains a professional reputation. Nor is this the "craft" that critics and philosophers so often oppose to "art," defining the one as mere skilled execution and the other as deep expression. The craft I have in mind involves a concentration on materials, not so much to fashion something already existing in thought, but to explore the material and physical world with an unrelenting intensity, causing a creatively invested fragment of that world to assume its distinctive form.

Jackson, Savage, and Warren respond to a situation close at hand.

They are artists of the studio. They share an absorption in the process of building things with deliberation and contemplation, letting things develop, attending to the way that materials not only respond to the pressures of the hand but also guide the hand, the eye, and the artist's thought. They demonstrate that artists — and potentially everyone — can concentrate or focus their being *through* materials in the way that poets concentrate their thoughts and emotions through words, especially during the very physical act of composing the words on paper, with the words assuming a material presence. For the visual artist, a mark of paint, an element of an assembled sculpture, or any other material component, becomes an expressive unit like the word, but free of the word's set of conventional references.

Visual artists thus assume a curious advantage over poets in that their forms exist only in a specific environment. Visual forms have no "dictionary"; they can be used as if they had never been used elsewhere before. In contrast to elements of painting and sculpture, the words that constitute a literary artifact have a standard orthography and bear preexisting circulated definitions; they have an abstract, dematerialized identity and seem to belong already to all speakers of the language. It is as if they have no visual style. To note this difference is not to say that an artist's visual elements must themselves be so novel that they fail to stir our collective memories and cannot carry familiar connotations along with them, just as words do. Nevertheless, marks of paint and shaped pieces of wood or metal are physical things which retain a special life in our commodity culture of reproducible symbols and images because we commonly regard these artistic elements, as well as their combinations, as possessing absolute specificity. If I publish my text in a variant typeface, I have still written the same essay. But if I change the color of my painting, or the finish on my sculpture, I have made a different work of art. This example does not hold without exception since it can easily be argued that the look or format of a text bears its own connotative meaning and alters the impact. Such an objection, however, merely borrows from the specificity of physical things, attributing some of their visuality to words, only to strengthen the initial claim of a difference.

It comes down to this: in our culture a certain form of communication, verbal communication, is awarded the privilege of maximum standardization, making it the most regulative and reliable. Accordingly, we set our laws into words, not pictures, on the assumption that the specific physicality of the ink and paper used in printing will not affect the meaning. Laws can be disseminated without much concern for the medium, regarding the various modes of publication as interchangeable. Although any use of words can be shown to generate an interminable and unpredictable set of meanings, it is perverse to insist on regarding ordinary forms of instructive or regulative language in this manner. To do so is to give up the law. In contrast, non-verbal forms of communication — either by default or by their very nature — assume the ultimate freedom that language, in its utilitarian circulation and by an implicit social contract, must lack. This explains why the word "art" evokes painting more readily than writing, although both are arts of creativity and skill. Colors may have been laid down by others and countless sculptural structures may already have been built, but never *these* structures occupying *this* space, or *this* patch of color *here* with *these* dimensions and *these* nuances. The visual is the specific; it constitutes a realm of imaginative innovation and needs to be reinvestigated every time it appears.

The type of art object made by Jackson, Savage, or Warren first concentrates its maker's attention and then its viewer's because its physicality has been intensified and engaged to hold a unique center. In this respect, the Davidson artists preserve a traditional sense of the ultimate impenetrability of unique hand-crafted objects. Such objects must be seen first-hand and perhaps touched. They cannot be paraphrased. Herb Jackson associates this quality with the much debated notion of "non-verbal thought." The works of Jackson, Savage, and Warren concentrate thought and feeling within a process of becoming. These works do not illustrate, but rather give form to — that is to say, they form in themselves, they constitute — experience.

HERB JACKSON

Herb Jackson refers to himself as a "gestural abstract painter." From a distance, the forms on his canvases resemble the sweeping gestures of the Abstract Expressionist generation, with all the liberated energy such visual motifs represent. One thinks perhaps of the late color paintings of Franz Kline or of de Kooning or Motherwell at their most expansive. Yet the characteristic movement of Jackson's arm is not especially broad and his painter's tools tend to be small — brushes of modest size, palette knives, and various instruments for scraping. Jackson intends his paintings to be seen at a distance, but it is just as important to him that they be inspected close up.

The field of his paintings can be quite large (**Dream of the Minotaur,** of 1988, reached 15 feet), yet Jackson works all his surfaces, large or small, to the finest detail. Among his artistic heroes is the collage artist Kurt Schwitters, a master of small-scale abstraction. When Jackson's viewer is close by the work, or listens closely to what the artist will say about that work, it becomes apparent that the method of composition involves a slow and deliberate process of layering, with a subsequent complementary process of scraping down or scratching out. The resultant structure is rather like those walls in European cities — Jackson often took note of them on his travels — that accumulate layer upon layer of brilliantly colored posters over a number of years. Eventually the walls are abandoned and become subject to weathering; wearing down, they endure the layering process in reverse. Fragments peel off to reveal contrasting fragments, with the wall becoming a complex collage of abstract shapes cutting into one another both visually and physically. Here, visual tensions exceed the psychological boundaries of familiar visual illusion because the viewer perceives a "real" conflict in materials. The very physical nature of this conflict is manifest: while one layer remains hidden by the masking effect of another, still another layer is revealed as a result of yet another's destruction (Jackson's **Vulcan's Gate** and **Dark Angel** pack this type of animated visual tension particularly tightly within their borders).

Like the wall marked by time, the surface of a Jackson painting is anything but smooth to the touch; the hand will feel its depressions, ridges, furrows, and incisions. To the eye, depressed areas of color with jagged edges look as if they have lost a layer to tearing. The paint edge appears deckled, similar to the edge of a piece of quality artist's paper, a material as familiar to Jackson as canvas; and the look of tearing, of course, also recalls collage. In his paintings, Jackson creates this "torn" effect by gradually working a scraped area out toward its expanding edges. Such a "gesture" can neither represent a single moment nor be accomplished at a single stroke; it is instead complex and laboriously achieved, composed of many adjustments to contour as the interior shape gradually grows and spreads. We discover a related type of gestural complexity in **All the Shadows Are Mine**, where a set of rather large parallel streaks or scratches at the center of the composition appears to have been caused by a single movement, as if the artist had dragged an oversized comb through wet pigment. Yet the fact is that Jackson constructed each of these wide incisions separately, only gradually building up the effect and only gradually determining its extent in response to other developing features of the same composition. And there is still more dramatic evidence of Jackson's commitment to purposeful construction: in the same work, the central violet shape continues beyond the framing edge; the artist has painted the sides of his stretched canvas, as if to recognize the physical continuity of front and side of the picture (this technique can be observed in each of his works in the exhibition). Like the nature and the earth that are among his painting's referents, the picture ends only where its materiality runs out. Since the framing sides of Jackson's "construction site" remain visible under actual conditions of exhibition (although unseen in reproduction), they must be painted as part of the work. In the same spirit Jackson also stains the top edge of his canvases so that they glow under studio or gallery illumination, suggesting that the material presence of a painting extends to the top as well as along the sides.

A characteristic painting by Jackson may have 50 to 100 distinct layers, becoming a kind of archaeological relic as well as a site of construction — or, to combine these two allusions, we might compare his work to an active archaeological site. Indeed, archaeology has been one of Jackson's fascinations, with his art having been inspired by numerous travels to Greece and the Mediterranean. We think of archaeologists digging into what others created long ago. Jackson, to the contrary, digs into his own accumulated gestures of painting, returning to moments of color that belong to a very recent past, a past composed of the days already devoted to the painting in progress (with its many shifts in orientation and composition, a typical work will consume about 200 hours of the artist's studio time).

"Digging" is not just a metaphor for Jackson but an apt description of his process: he usually adds pumice or mica to his paints in order to provide texture and substance; to his synthetic acrylic-based pigments, he thus adds pieces of the natural earth (not surprisingly, he admires the French painter Jean Dubuffet, who had a related sense of materials). Dried acrylic paint forms a durable surface; the added pumice, or the mica, affords a sufficiently tough physicality to the entirety of the painting (whether wet or dry) so that the artist can cut and strip parts of it away. Pumice also offers a matte appearance (whereas mica glistens like hard coal), and this gives the work an earthen or weathered look. Again, one thinks of archaeology. A striking result of Jackson's technique is to be seen in the black areas of **Presence of the Other** where the mineral-like, material quality of the pigment suggests a vein in the earth as well as an artist's constructed gesture. And in **Anchor** the dark enframing area at the upper right, composed of pearlescent violet pigment and mica added to black, produces a richly textured violet-black, a color unusual enough to leave the viewer wondering whether it belongs to a painter's studio or to nature's depository. As Jackson converts his synthetic plastic paints into mineral compounds (whether by actual addition of minerals or by the connotations of his preferred colors), he acts upon a realization — he is, as he states, "happier in nature than in cities." Accordingly, his abstract paintings become lyrical landscapes even when square in format, homages to nature and attempts at enjoining natural processes: "I consider my work as a part of nature, rather than a statement about nature."

Having developed a distinctive set of studio practices, Jackson performs his archaeological labor in specific ways. Taken together, his practices constitute a meditation or ritual that induces deep states of concentration in which both mental and physical forms of attentiveness become acute. Jackson often digs into surfaces still wet with paint by using a "palette" knife (more precisely, a painting knife, a small trowel-like device designed for applying paint as a paste). He also accomplishes his digging, especially when the paint has dried, by using sharp engraver's tools, sticks, and even his fingernails. Some of the digging amounts to a scratching (such as the bold yet deliberative striations in **All the Shadows Are Mine**, already mentioned). The scratches may reveal a contrasting color underneath or simply remain incisions on a relatively monochrome surface (both effects are to be found in the central violet area of **Anchor**). These calculated reductions to a painting's surface evoke rock carving and other types of sculptural relief imagery; as in relief work, the subtractive markings become as expressive as any additive strokes. This is to say that Jackson's self-contained archaeological venture, as he first builds up and then cuts into and strips away, retains his personal identity and a productive expressiveness at all stages of the procedure. Clearly, he has his own unique ways of drawing and painting by digging into a painting surface; the subtractions are in no sense corrections, but

rather an essential part of a continuous process. Jackson even adds new layers of color to some of the areas stripped away, constructing his work as a play of opposing impulses and directions. His gestures can be either positive or negative; the difference is physical and not necessarily psychological since both types of gesture constitute the nature of the expressive process.

Rather than conceive his composition in advance, Jackson finds it through this back-and-forth movement. As he states, "I make no attempt to save or protect any area of the painting [from digging away] unless it seems necessary to the life of the whole." True to a modernist conception of the value of spontaneity, Jackson adds that at a certain point in the developing experience, the canvas itself determines the direction the painter must take. So spontaneity for this painter is not in a sweep of the arm, a flick of the wrist, or a twist of the brush. It lies instead in the artist's openness and sensitivity to what the material construction before his eyes may suggest as an appropriate turn of events.

As I have argued, events and changes of direction in Jackson's imaginative world — a world of experience concentrated on the painting at hand — can be traced to his effects of layering. And they can be traced to other effects as well. Jackson's use of subtle complementary glazes allows areas of color to shift before the viewer's eyes, making it nearly impossible to identify the local color by the usual descriptive terms. The color can be clearly enough seen, but designating it and its strange qualities in words becomes a conundrum (I'll attempt a brief description in a moment).

Perhaps this visual effect is the literal proof of Jackson's principle of the "non-verbal." He speaks of making decisions "in response to the emerging painting, and they are determined non-verbally, so that it is possible to have a session lasting several hours without a verbal thought." In other words, the painter does not think "now it's time to do the green"; instead, under his painting hand, unique configurations of color assume unforeseen qualities to be considered only after the fact of their existence. The painter must judge whether such qualities are desirable. This is his "non-verbal" decision, and it will lead to either enhancement or obliteration of the curious effects in question. In **Core**, for instance, a large shape at the right appears as a dull violet, yet green also makes its presence felt as both layered glazes and scrapings; this green veers toward yellow-green because of the influence of the violet that shares the same field. I can only say that the shape appears violet and green simultaneously — not violet *and* or *with* green, but something that is both and neither of these colors. Another example is the dark, blackish area at the left edge of **Anchor**; one cannot deny this blackness, yet a variable white glazing contributes a curiously ethereal character to what ought to appear, but no longer appears, opaque like densely packed soil. Such effects apparently intrigued the artist, who cultivated them.

To conceive of Jackson's work as a self-investigative archaeology is to associate it with introspection and personal memory. The time span of the work is Jackson's own; the layers covered and unconvered in a painting belong to the artist's life experience and emotions. A more general mythology is evoked through the archaeological conceit itself (since mythology and archaeology share the world of ancient Greece) and perhaps also through the vaguely Mediterranean color, brilliant but muted, like the stuccoed surfaces of contemporary Greece or the remains of Pompeian frescoes. Indeed, the painter

became interested in ancient myth at an early age and remains affected by it (to which his titles bear witness). Yet, the content of Jackson's myth never becomes explicit; and perhaps only the artist will ever know the specific thoughts associated with a given work and its period of active creation in the studio.

Despite all this, Jackson does not consider himself and his art self-centered, in the sense of being without any general social relevance. Appropriate to his role as a teacher, he (like Warren and Savage) believes that artistic activity constitutes a running commentary on the conditions of society, as well as fostering an enhanced sense of human nature and human potential. Jackson's paintings are meant to concern people as well as refer to nature. The analogy is obvious enough: formed by layers of experience, people, like nature, become subjects for the archaeologist; they become, as Jackson puts it, "collages."

CORT SAVAGE

Because his father practiced carpentry, Cort Savage grew up familiar with craft, daily labor, and the nature of common tools and building materials. He is something of a bricoleur or handyman, and very much at home in a studio environment arranged more like a small custom manufacturer's workshop than a fine artist's atelier.

Savage is a protean inventor, but it is as if his workshop were lacking pragmatic orientation, specific assignment, or conceivable consumer market. His strangely "manufactured" items, each piece one of a kind, evoke familiar household appliances and furnishings, but subvert rather than confirm the American ideal of technological economy and efficiency. Savage's manufactures have a vaguely makeshift quality to them, with many of his component parts having been salvaged from the discards of commerce or everyday use. This uniqueness lends to each assemblage and construction the unsettling sense that it may be a prototype for others. Will there be a series of such things, each a bit closer to perfecting the design and eventually rendering obvious what purpose the product might actually serve? Perhaps one experimental item is being derived from another in Savage's factory for technological monsters, each creation realizing its domesticated application and function only partially. When you enter the fantasy world of Savage's studio you imagine yourself privileged to see the inventive "prototypes" well before they are ready to be released into the human environment of mass consumption.

Savage directs his handyman's tools and his considerable knowledge of mechanical and electrical engineering to create rather humorous, but mildly threatening motorized sculptures. The movements these devices perform seem pointless, yet capture and hold a viewer's attention. Because the movements repeat only at extended intervals, viewers can neither assess nor dismiss their effects quickly. Not only does the movement make no sense in terms of mechanical efficiency, but the scope of its interaction with the viewer's environment and its cumulative force remain indeterminate. The movements of Savage's constructions have their own regularity, but it is strange enough to confuse a viewer's expectations.

One would be tempted to categorize Savage's artworks as installations because of their interactive complexity; **A Looming**, for instance, induces the viewer to sit on a chair which forms part of the total construction. Savage prefers to use the more comprehensive designation "sculpture" as opposed to the specialized term "installation"; although his works may demand from the viewer some active bodily engagement (as when you walk into and through the space of an installation piece), the more basic effect of Savage's art is to extend the sensory apparatus normally brought into play by a sculptural presence. Savage activates his viewer's sensations in a particularly compelling way because the kinetic aspect of his creations is more than just visual: each object's movements not only captivate the eye but also make specific sounds essential to the intended effect. Indeed, sounds often concentrate human attention much more than visual appearances since one cannot fully turn away from sound — sound surrounds and insinuates itself. Curiously, and perhaps paradoxically, Savage's sounds verge on silence. Listen to the gently clacking clatter of **A Looming** as you sit within its space; discern the muffled harmonic tones generated by the speaker-like forms of **Dürer**; be distracted by the quiet pop and bounce of the projectiles issuing from **Pseudoscience and Baby Toys** or by the whir of the **Insufflator**; try to follow the hum of **Turn in Silence** (certainly a significant title) or the voiceless roll of the rubber cord in **Probiscidea**.

If a particular visual trope characterizes all of Savage's work, that device is the juxtaposition of forms and materials so opposed in their connotations that the effect is nonsensical or absurd. In **A Looming** a large canopy covered with a patterned, textured blue-green fabric hovers over a not entirely inviting chair; beside the chair, and suspended from the canopy, hangs a set of pocketknife blades. The hard shiny blades rise and fall intermittently, tapping against the floor to produce a brittle metallic clatter; they contrast with the soft and stable fabric surface above. Yet, as the viewer attends to the seemingly random movements of the blades, he or she is likely also to keep glancing apprehensively at the oversized canopy — it is so heavy in appearance that it may well assume more of a presence than the blades, tiny by comparison. As the title's reference to "looming" suggests, the canopy resembles an ominous thundercloud as much as an overstuffed couch; it threatens to fall or descend because its shape, anvil-like yet upholstered, lends it great visual weight. This massive softness could just as well crush or stifle as comfort.

Savage's inventions are fantastic and monstrous combinations. Expressively ambiguous, they solicit a double response of laughter and terror; you don't know whether to be amused or threatened by their movements and sounds, a kind of weird science. Actually, the effect is usually subtler than my reference to fantastic monsters may make it seem. Consider **Turn in Silence**, which consists of a wooden chest of three large drawers pierced by a slowly turning tubular steel ring, driven by a hidden motor. You are perhaps amused by the illogic of this performing steel hoop; but, puzzled, you cannot quite smile over what you see because the joke, if there is one, escapes you (what can this turning really be about?). A cryptic inscription, carved into the top of the dresser, may or may not help: "A tree best echoes when hollowed." Is the hollowness of the drawers what makes the kinetic regularity of the steel ring possible? Does the structure of the ring act as a lock on the drawers, rendering the dresser non-functional? If instead of amusement, you feel vaguely threatened by the presence of some mysterious force responsible for the turning, you are unlikely to experience real fright, but will perhaps instead feel what Savage himself associates with his works — a sense of "dread." To put it

irreverently, Savage's sculptures are both comical and creepy. You have one response, then the other. Perhaps this is a roundabout way of realizing that Savage's art, his technological horror show, produces not monsters but wonder.

Savage's creations most always employ domestic decorative motifs as one of their essential elements. The worn-out and rather basic wooden dresser of **Turn in Silence** is hardly decorative in the sense of being ornamented, but it surely connotes a familiar kind of American home environment (decoration by salvage operation). More typically, as in **A Looming** or **Dürer** or **Probiscidea**, Savage's "domestic" element is a gently curving form covered with patterned or velour fabric, connoting somewhat old-fashioned upholstered furniture and appointments. These fabric surfaces either assume the form of or become elements of large structures reminiscent of heavy machinery or even armaments. Given this alienating combination of the signs of both domesticity and heavy industry, the material juxtapositions become as jarring as the formal ones. In **Pseudoscience and Baby Toys** (again, the title itself says a great deal) steel ribbing surrounds pastel flannel-covered panels, with all parts contributing to an object that in its general form resembles a vintage atom bomb; yet this device does no more than harmlessly shoot out blue handballs to the sound I've described as a gentle pop and bounce. **Pseudoscience and Baby Toys** combines two senses of scale, absurdly: as a plaything, it should be small enough to be handled by an infant; as a bomb, it should be large enough to cause some damage. If a weapon, the device unexpectedly shoots only small, bouncy projectiles, so that this large threatening object is reduced in its kinetic activity to the function of a harmless toy (and the toy is *slow* — it is programmed to shoot one ball every ten minutes for a total of one hundred balls; it thus provides nearly seventeen hours of uneventful action). This tension and shift in scale and power is what may well provoke a viewer's gentle laugh, for the oversize device — itself shaped like a projectile — does nothing other than dribble out bouncing balls at a pace so retarded you may not realize a second missile is ever to follow the first. Savage has added another realm of association to the toy and the weapon by stating — I do not know how deliberately — that the action of his device is to "excrete" balls, as opposed to "ejecting" or "propelling" them. Since excretion connotes organic, bodily functions more than mechanical ones, **Pseudoscience and Baby Toys** suddenly also assumes the form of a living organism. Perhaps it can represent a giant flannel-covered baby (or some other willful being) as well as the baby's environment and the baby's toy.

Indeed, Savage's work is not without reference to the body and its actions. An intriguing example is his **Insufflator**; unlike most of the artist's other creations and despite its pliant form (like a hinge or a roll of flexible material), this object gives no obvious appearance of performing a movement. That is to say, its movement cannot be *seen*. Yet movement there must be, because we hear it in a subtle whirring sound resembling that of a vacuum cleaner. The material and physical presence of the **Insufflator** itself evokes mechanical vacuuming not only because the work lies low on the floor, but because its most obvious components are rubber matting and a velvet fabric much like carpeting. Unlike household vacuums, this device appears to do little if any physical work; its two visible air vents (intake and output) do no more than send periodic flows of heated air upward toward the observer's face, where such warmth is most readily felt. You imagine at first that a motor is operating and giving off a warm exhaust; then you gradually realize that this "exhaust" is

the device's primary product, not a by-product. Savage's invention seems rather elaborate given its limited output. The "meaning," of course, lies not in what labor the **Insufflator** can accomplish but in what it does to one's imagination. Its organic, involuted forms evoke a living presence; like a human or animal body, it seems to have an inside that opens onto its outside and an outside that turns into its inside. The most "living" part of the **Insufflator** may be the warmth issuing forth from it, a kind of breath. The designation "insufflator" itself provides some degree of resolution to Savage's conceptual puzzle since it alludes to insufflation, a breathing or blowing into or on another person, with connotations of both divine inspiration and rituals of Christian exorcism. Is this homely device actually a rare machine for exorcising domestic demons? Or does it represent a threat of its own, industrial design coming too close to life?

Each of Savage's inventions evokes a certain nostalgia for the typically mechanical domestic environment of the mid-twentieth century, that collection of metallic, motorized devices and appliances imposed upon a somewhat older world of stuffed chairs, carpets, and drapes. The characteristically modern appliances — identified with the rapid advance of American consumer industry — might once have stirred the consciousnesses of a Siegfried Giedion or a Buckminster Fuller as they imagined what life would be like in the home of the near future. Born in 1965, Savage inherited that future and many things beyond it. Members of his generation have been living through an age more electronic than mechanical; for them, it is certainly time to take retrospective stock of the mythologies of the age of domestic mechanization — that alliance of home life and heavy industry, with all its attendant quirkiness. Savage's method of investigation is to alienate the viewer from the normal comforts of domestic environments and familiar materials and technologies. His creations constitute a fantasia on the theme of life in the American home and workplace.

RUSS WARREN

If Cort Savage's concentration lies in his astute choice of materials and the intense care he takes in designing the mechanisms of his technological (or anti-technological) wonders, Russ Warren's concentration, much like Herb Jackson's, appears in the form of densely packed painted surfaces. Warren, however, creates narrative images, not abstractions. Yet, as in Jackson's case, Warren's work exhibits its concentrated artistic energy independent of whatever external events and situations the painter may be representing. There is a sense in which Warren, even as he devotes himself to folk imagery, remains an "abstract" artist — one who attends to the physical order of his materials and the configurations they often seem to produce quite naturally, forms which the artist *feels*, as much as sees, through the process of creating them by hand.

Warren's work readily attracts two different types of observation. Since his paintings tell stories, a certain kind of viewer will want to decipher the subject matter. **Latané**, for instance, concerns Warren's Southern heritage; it represents a funeral scene and refers to the legend of the first Confederate officer to die in the war, who was buried by his family and a slave. Since Warren's narrative paintings also manifest a very distinctive craft and sense of composition, another kind of viewer will prefer to inspect the artist's application of pigment. Warren's characteristic handling involves small

overlapping, sweeping gestures which produce a fine texture. He has stated that an understanding of the place of texture in painting came to him initially from depictions of the Old West by Frederick Remington, seen at the Houston Museum of Fine Arts. Warren's distinctive textures may nevertheless cause a viewer to think of a dense weaving or even a patterned animal skin rather than of Remington or any other studio painter. Indeed, it seems that Warren's work, like Jackson's, induces features of human craft and of nature to converge in the viewer's imagination.

Each aspect of Warren's work — the cryptic subject matter and the dense, richly patterned pigment — influences the other. The artist tells his stories as much with color and design as with the invention of appropriate figures (among his primitivistic renderings are historical folk heroes, rural laborers, and prize horses). Warren explains that as his formal composition emerges, it determines the specific details of the figures he is in the midst of creating. Ever since Cézanne and Matisse, this kind of spontaneous pictorial feedback has been an aim to which modernist artists have aspired. In Warren's case, however, this understanding of composition needs to be connected with a folk tradition as well as with the modernist development toward abstraction.

Warren was deeply affected during his early student years around 1970-1971 by his encounter with the work of the Chicago "imagists" (Jim Nutt, Roger Brown, and H. C. Westermann are perhaps the best known). These painters and sculptors turned away from the abstract modes then in vogue — color-field painting and large-scale steel construction — in order to create a style deliberately regional and "popular" (in the sense of being derived from mass culture). Their style represented a combination of naive folk imagery and cartoon-like urban graphics, often executed in the garish saturated colors typical of comic strips and magazine advertising. At about the same time Warren also became familiar with the California version of this resistance to the modernist avant-garde, as seen in the alternative offered by Roy de Forest. But Warren came from Texas, with all his education conducted in Texas and New Mexico. So he naturally compared what was happening in Chicago and California to what he saw around him. Indeed, the imagery of Texas artists was beginning to look somewhat similar, but, Warren thought, it had a "rural" feel to it, not the stridency and caustic irony of big-city Chicago or California art. Warren recognized that he himself was "rural." Part of that sense came from the Southwestern and Mexican folk traditions with which he had grown up and identified. He had always admired the colorful, inexpensive Mexican dresses sold in Texas shops and the wood carving practiced as a rural craft throughout the region.

The confluence of elements of traditional Southwestern craft and "rural" folk imagery and myth is evident in nearly all of Warren's work. His composition **Don't Be Lazy** serves as an especially telling example. The title refers to the fact that farmers work from dawn to dusk. Indeed, Warren depicts his figures in exaggerated, unrealistic postures that suggest extremely vigorous action, as if he were designing a poster image that needed to be legible from a great distance — not across a boulevard but across a prairie. His figures have the simplicity and expressive linearity we associate with various types of naive rendering; the curve of the arched back of the man waving the sickle, for instance, extends as a continuous motif downward into the line of that figure's leg and upward along the arm. The figure becomes, in effect, an element of an integrated expressive

pattern. Its structure of thin, rather brittle curves and angles finds an echo not only in the form of the sickle itself, but elsewhere in the similar lines and curves of the plantings, the furrows, and even the patterned clouds. This patterned integration goes still further, since the design of the clouds stands as a horizontal counterpart to the vertical furrows, just as the angularity of the left-hand figure's pitchfork contrasts with the curve of the right-hand figure's sickle. It is not difficult to imagine how the various forms fell into place as Warren gradually elaborated on the composition of his basic concept.

In **Don't Be Lazy** "craft" is signified doubly: first, in the ordered labor of the farm hands themselves; second, in the details of pattern and textural overlay that mark this painting as a finely honed hand-made object, itself the product of a dawn-to-dusk labor as intense as that of its depicted rural workers. Warren directs and concentrates the viewer's attention upon the smallest marks within his relatively large painting: the thin, lightly colored veins in the dark plant forms; the dots of pigment that here represent seeds (compare the similar motif beneath the slave's spade in **Latané**); and, finally, the short strokes of paint that depict no particular thing but simply constitute the constructive nuances of each area of coloring. The variety of all these marks, and their precise placement, are indications of the painter's own highly developed craft, while they also evoke a quality of detail and precision typically found in objects of folk art. Varied repetition of a decorative motif — as in the case of the generic plant form Warren uses to represent growing crops — is itself a recognizable sign of a folk art tradition. It is difficult to sort out when and where Warren is imitating "naive" or folk practices and when he is simply employing them because they actually seem the most natural and comfortable to him. The critical viewer's difficulty arises because

Warren is so genuinely involved with his materials and with acts of painstaking craftsmanship like those of the rural carvers and weavers he admires. That he would ever shift his mode of painting to one less dependent on a disciplined and caring hand seems highly unlikely.

While Warren may have turned back to folk traditions as an inspiration and justification for his painting style and process, he also turned to the one European tradition most closely associated with the American Southwest and with Mexico — Spanish art, both in its baroque manifestations from Velazquez and Zurbaràn through Goya and in its modern appearance in Picasso. From the baroque and from Goya, Warren derived effects of dramatic lighting and abrupt diagonal recession. An example is **Burial at Barrio San Antonio**, the artist's homage to Goya, in which he reconstructs a mysterious legend, the belief that Goya himself was buried "headless" in the town of Barrio San Antonio. Warren interprets the story with his intentionally "naive," folkish wit — we see two golden angels beside a coffin carrying on a plate a severed head, presumably Goya's. The same motif is repeated several times to the right, with red demons performing the action.

Warren derived some of his use of strong compositional oppositions from Goya, but even more of them from Picasso's graphic works, with their abrupt shifts of lighting, tonality, and linear density. Striking formal oppositions create the visual order needed to support themes such as heaven versus hell or angel versus demon, as seen in **Burial at Barrio San Antonio**. It is by no means surprising that similar oppositions appear in the work **Images From Heaven and Hell**. Aspects of the style of this painting may belong to Picasso, but its title is part imagination and part Mozart — Warren was listening to

that composer's Requiem mass during the entire time he worked on this project. The fantastic winged figure at the upper left of **Images From Heaven and Hell**, which recalls an angel of the Annunciation, issues a golden stream to be interpreted as either light or voice (perhaps it is a "stream" of Mozart). The zone of the angel contrasts dramatically with what, at the bottom right, appears to be the dark zone of Hell, peopled by Warren's familiar fiery red creatures. Much of the painting's surface is filled with bulbous volumetric forms, resembling both rocks and clouds (mammatus clouds have precisely this shape, but upside down); as they shift from rose pink to pale blue, these forms effect a pictorial passage from one zone to another without necessarily signifying any real objects. With his extreme attentiveness, even obsessiveness, Warren develops variation within this repetitive pattern (note the great variety of size and shape among what are essentially similar elements).

As in **Don't Be Lazy**, Warren's patterned forms constitute a genuine, highly personalized craft as well as a contemporary artist's representation or reworking of a continuing folk tradition, one particularly hospitable to the reinsertion of certain European formal devices (dramatic color contrasts and bold "baroque" compositions). Like Mexican folk variants of Spanish prototypes, Warren's simplified figures and compositions lack a detailed naturalism yet exhibit intensive decorative detailing. The artist repeats "abstract" formal motifs so that they generate a vitality of their own, through their own variation and visual interest. This is the essence of Warren's "abstraction," a concentration and intensification of the physicality of his paint and its inherent visual energy.

Most recently, Warren's narratives have been fantasies concerning prize horses, the Paso Fino breed he and his family raise at their farm Locura East. **Fino, Fino Por Favor** and **Belleza Hoy Dia, Fino Mañana** depict events at horse shows in Asheville, North Carolina. The word "fino" refers to the special gait the horses perform naturally, which produces a distinctively rhythmic sound as the animal moves across the wooden planks of a walkway; this detail can be seen in the foreground of **Fino, Fino Por Favor**. In this image, Warren enframes the horse with an aura of red and gold concentric bands, each containing silhouettes of gesticulating figures. These are the Latin horse trainers, located in the circular rows of an arena. Warren offers this suggestion of perspective (the horse being "surrounded" or "within" the receding space of a circle or oval) and combines it with a "flat" background pattern (the small human figures appearing sufficiently similar in scale so as to deny perspective recession). The resultant tension between the predominant flat pattern and the hint of deep space is characteristic of "naive" or folk illustration.

Each element of Warren's folk narrative assumes a particularly iconic or sign-like quality. In **Fino, Fino Por Favor** the prize horse's ribbon, an essential part of the story, seems suspended below the horse, occupying a central position in the picture in accord with its significance. "Behind" the ribbon, the horse, and the wooden walkway lies a graphic hint of the mountains of Asheville, an iconic way of identifying the region in which the depicted event occurs. Ultimately, Warren's sense of patterned composition determines the placement of these various narrative elements. The location of the schematically depicted mountains corresponds to the perspective of the receding planks of the walkway; the mountains become a horizontal band which arrests the eye's movement "back" into space. From these two narrative incidents (the walkway and the mountains) Warren creates a single visual motif. This coordinated effect has its counterpart in **Belleza Hoy Dia, Fino Mañana** where diagonal paths of light pass from the background stable so that they parallel the foreground Paso Fino's rear legs, joining these two pictorial details in one integrated visual rhythm.

Warren's sense of design is so much a part of his life that it sometimes threatens to displace practical, utilitarian considerations. When the artist needed to paint a roadside sign for visitors to Locura East, he felt an urge to make the lettering brown in order to match the adjacent fence; this would have been harmonious, of course, but, lacking strong color contrast, would have failed to attract the passing driver's eye. Warren's patterned narrative paintings of horses and folk legends are quite another matter — their concentrated craft catches all eyes in the vicinity.

—Richard Shiff

HERB JACKSON

BORN: Raleigh, North Carolina, USA 1945

EDUCATION: B.A. Davidson College 1967
Philips Universität, Marburg, Germany
M.F.A. University of North Carolina, Chapel Hill 1970

Selected Solo Exhibitions:
Jerald Melberg Gallery, Charlotte, NC '84,'85,'87,'88,'90,'91,'93
Phyllis Weil & Co., New York, NY '81,'83,'84,'87,'88,'90
Fay Gold Gallery, Atlanta, GA '86,'88,'92
Impressions Gallery, Boston, MA '75,'77,'81
Allene Lapides Gallery, Santa Fe, NM '89,'90
Christa Faut Gallery, Davidson, NC '90,'93
Peden Gallery II, Raleigh, NC '91,'93
Oxford Gallery, Oxford, England '82
Judy Youens Gallery, Houston, TX '88
Mint Museum of Art, Charlotte, NC '73,'83
National Academy of Sciences, Washington, DC '83
Fundacao Calouste Gulbenkian, Lisbon, Portugal '84
Edmonton Art Gallery, Edmonton, Alberta, Canada '85
St. John's Museum of Art, Wilmington, NC '93
Hickory Museum of Art, Hickory, NC '93

Selected Group Exhibitions:
Knoxville Museum of Art, Knoxville, TN '91
Samuel P. Harn Museum of Art, Gainesville, FL '90
Kuznetsky Most Exhibition Hall, Moscow, Russia '89
Lorenzelli Arte, Milan, Italy '89
American Academy and Institute of Arts and Letters, New York, NY '81, '87
Southeastern Center for Contemporary Art, Winston-Salem, NC '75, '79, '83, '85, '87
Palazzo Venezia, Rome, Italy '84
VIII International Transpersonal Association Conference, Davos, Switzerland '83
XV International São Paulo Bienal, São Paulo, Brazil '79

ANCHOR
Acrylic on canvas 1991
84 x 144

VULCAN'S GATE
Acrylic on canvas 1989
102 x 132

ALL THE SHADOWS ARE MINE
Acrylic on canvas 1992
72 x 72

CORE
Acrylic on canvas 1989
66 x 90

PRESENCE OF THE OTHER
Acrylic on canvas 1992
84 x 120

DARK ANGEL
Acrylic on canvas 1991
84 x 84

CORT SAVAGE

BORN: Hammond, Indiana, USA 1965

EDUCATION: B.A. Indiana University, Bloomington, IN 1987
M.F.A. Syracuse University, Syracuse, NY 1991

Selected Solo Exhibitions:
Sculpture Space, Utica, NY '92
The Gertrude Thomas Chapman Art Center Gallery, Cazenovia, NY '91
Mohawk Valley College Cultural Center, Utica, NY '90
Rome Art Center, Rome, NY '90
Smith Hall Gallery, Syracuse, NY '90
Another Gallery, Syracuse, NY '88

Selected Juried Exhibitions:
Chapman Art Gallery, Cazenovia, NY '92
Barret House, Poughkeepsie, NY '90
Canal Town Museum, Canastota, NY '90
Chautauqua Art Association, Chautauqua, NY '90
Memorial Art Gallery, Rochester, NY '90
Pleiades Gallery, New York, NY '89
Munson William Proctor Institute Museum of Art, Utica, NY '89
Del Mar College, Corpus Christi, TX '89
Arnot Art Museum, Elmira, NY '88

Selected Group Exhibitions:
Mission Landing, Franklin Square, Syracuse, NY '91
12 Bedrooms and 2 Baths Gallery, Syracuse, NY '91
Schaffer Art Building, Syracuse, NY '90
Dowd Fine Arts Gallery, Cortland, NY '89
Delaware County College, Media, PA '89
Virginia Commonwealth University, Richmond, VA '89
Hartwick College, Oneonta, NY '89
Southwest Missouri State University, Springfield, MO '89
University of Nebraska, Lincoln, NE '89
University of Tennesee, Knoxville, TN '89
Comart Gallery, Syracuse, NY '88

PROBISCIDEA
Wood, velvet, rubber, electronics 1992
80 x 24 x 36

TURN IN SILENCE
Dresser, steel, motor 1992
42 x 45 x 60

DÜRER
Wood, fabric, steel, electronics, sound recording 1992
60 x 30 x 42

A LOOMING

Wood, fabric, chair, electronics, pocketknife blades 1992

108 x 30 x 144

PSEUDOSCIENCE AND BABY TOYS
Steel, wood, flannel, electronics, handballs 1991
88 x 48 x 48

INSUFFLATOR
Steel, rubber mat, velvet, heater/blower, electronics 1990
40 x 30 x 25

RUSS WARREN

BORN: Washington, D.C., USA 1951

EDUCATION: B.F.A. University of New Mexico, Albuquerque, NM 1973
M.F.A. University of Texas at San Antonio, TX 1977

Selected Solo Exhibitions:
Phyllis Kind Gallery, New York, NY '81,'82,'84
Phyllis Kind Gallery, Chicago, IL '84,'88
Knight Gallery, Charlotte, NC '84
North Carolina Museum of Art, Raleigh, NC '85
Hodges Taylor Gallery, Charlotte, NC '86,'88,'89,'91
Jerald Melberg Gallery, Charlotte, NC '84
Christa Faut Gallery, Davidson, NC '92

Selected Group Exhibitions:
Amerika Haus, Cologne, Germany '91
41'st Corcoran Biennial Exhibition of American Painting, Washington, DC '88,'90
1984 Venice Biennale, Venice, Italy '84
Palazzo Venezia, Rome, Italy '85
Contemporary Arts Museum, Houston, Texas '83
Virginia Museum, Richmond, VA '83
Indianapolis Museum of Art, Indianapolis, IN '82
Contemporary Arts Center, New Orleans, LA '82
Whitney Museum of American Art, New York, NY '81
New Orleans Museum of Art, New Orleans, LA '75,'80
Beaumont Art Museum, Beaumont, TX '75
Albright-Knox Gallery, Buffalo, NY '81

BURIAL AT BARRIO SAN ANTONIO
Acrylic on canvas 1987
60 x 90

IMAGES FROM HEAVEN AND HELL
Acrylic on canvas 1986
60 x 90

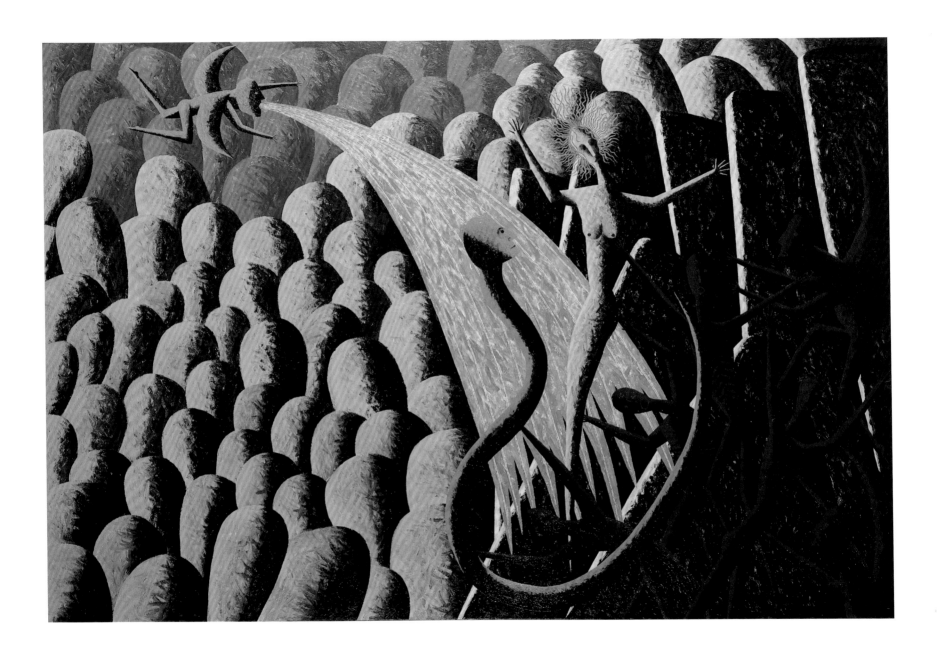

LATANÉ
Acrylic on canvas 1988
60 x 72

DON'T BE LAZY
Acrylic on canvas 1988
60 x 72

BELLEZA HOY DIA, FINO MAÑANA
Acrylic on canvas 1991
60 x 72

FINO FINO POR FAVOR
Acrylic on canvas   1991
60 x 72

CREDITS

Photographs of paintings by Bill Moretz
Photographs of sculpture by Mitchell Kearney
Photographs of artists by Bill Giduz
Design and production by Amber James

William H. Van Every, Jr. Gallery
Davidson College Visual Arts Center
Post Office Box 1720
Davidson, North Carolina 28036